W9-CAV-370

PLANETS

URANUS

Alexis Roumanis

www.av2books.com

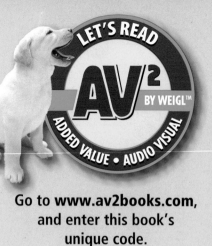

AV² provides enriched content that supplements and complements this book. Weigl's AV² books strive to create inspired learning and engage young minds in a total learning experience.

Your AV² Media Enhanced books come alive with...

 Audio
Listen to sections of the book read aloud.

 Video
Watch informative video clips.

 Embedded Weblinks
Gain additional information for research.

 Try This!
Complete activities and hands-on experiments.

 Key Words
Study vocabulary, and complete a matching word activity.

Quizzes
Test your knowledge.

Slide Show
View images and captions, and prepare a presentation.

... and much, much more!

Go to **www.av2books.com**, and enter this book's unique code.

BOOK CODE

T762645

AV² by Weigl brings you media enhanced books that support active learning.

Published by AV² by Weigl
350 5ᵗʰ Avenue, 59ᵗʰ Floor New York, NY 10118
Websites: www.av2books.com   www.weigl.com

Library of Congress Cataloging-in-Publication Data

Roumanis, Alexis, author.
 Uranus / Alexis Roumanis.
   pages cm. -- (Planets)
 Includes index.
 ISBN 978-1-4896-3304-0 (hard cover : alk. paper) -- ISBN 978-1-4896-3305-7 (soft cover : alk. paper) -- ISBN 978-1-4896-3306-4 (single user ebook) -- ISBN 978-1-4896-3307-1 (multi-user ebook)
 1. Uranus (Planet)--Juvenile literature. I. Title.
 QB681.R68 2016
 523.47--dc23
                              2014041543

Printed in the United States of America in Brainerd, Minnesota
1 2 3 4 5 6 7 8 9 0 19 18 17 16 15

022015
WEP081214

Project Coordinator: Katie Gillespie Art Director: Terry Paulhus

Weigl acknowledges Getty Images and iStock as the primary image suppliers for this title.

URANUS

CONTENTS

2 AV² Book Code
4 What Is Uranus?
6 How Big Is Uranus?
8 What Is Uranus Made Of?
10 What Does Uranus Look Like?
12 What Are Uranus's Rings?
14 What Are Uranus's Moons?
16 Who Discovered Uranus?
18 How Is Uranus Different from Earth?
20 How Do We Learn about Uranus Today?
22 Uranus Facts
24 Key Words/Log on to www.av2books.com

What Is Uranus?

Uranus is a planet. It moves in a path around the Sun. Uranus is the seventh planet from the Sun.

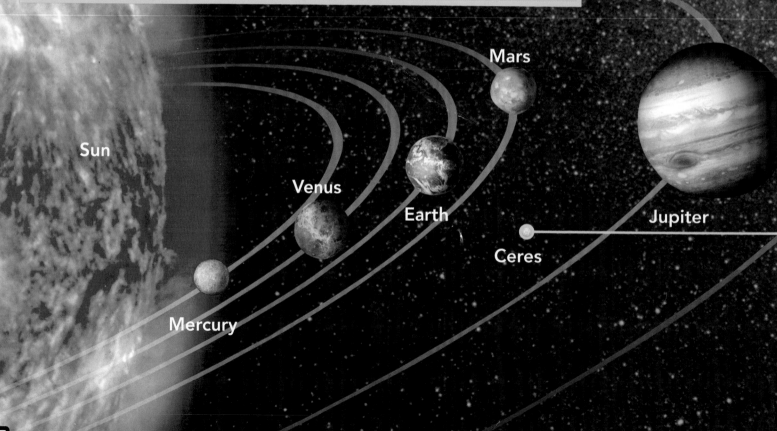

Sun

Mercury

Venus

Earth

Mars

Ceres

Jupiter

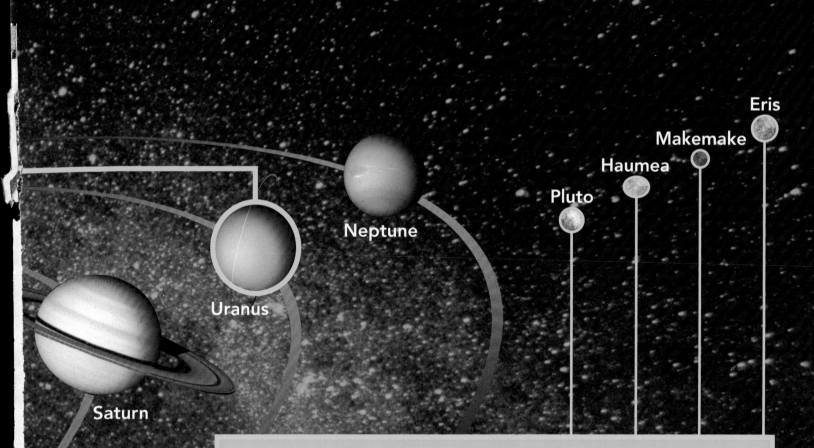

Eris

Makemake

Haumea

Pluto

Neptune

Uranus

Saturn

Dwarf Planets

Dwarf planets are round objects that move around the Sun. Unlike planets, they share their part of space with other objects.

How Big Is Uranus?

Uranus is the third largest planet in the solar system. It is almost four times as wide as Earth.

Uranus

Earth

What Is Uranus Made Of?

Uranus is a large planet made of ice. It is called an ice giant. Uranus also has a liquid center.

9

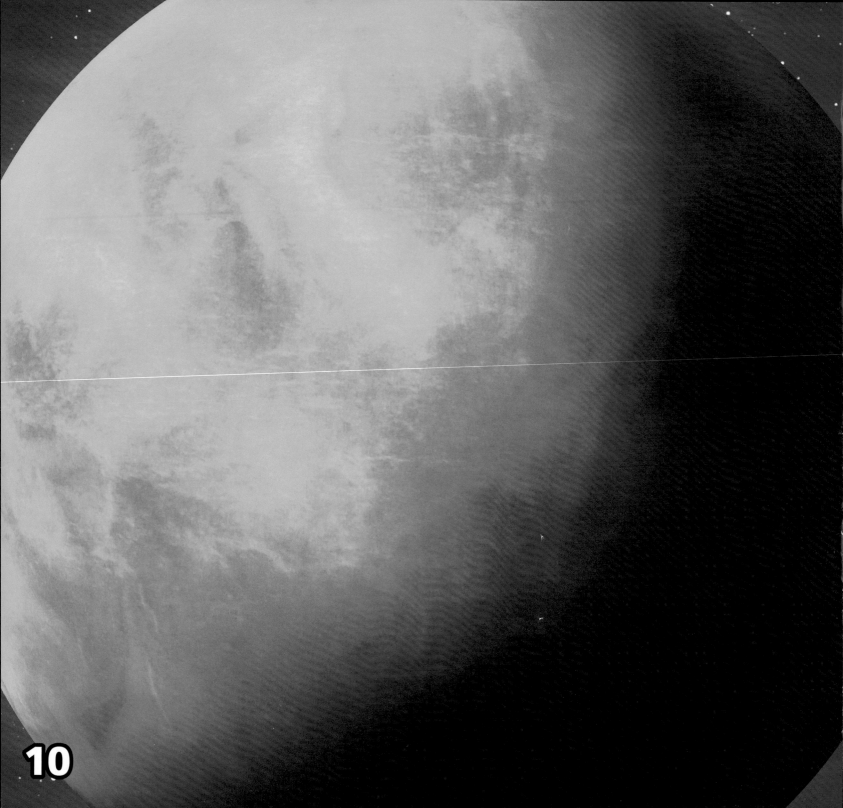

What Does Uranus Look Like?

Uranus looks bright blue. Gas clouds give the planet its color. Up close, these gas clouds look like stripes.

What Are Uranus's Rings?

Rings make circles around Uranus. They are made of ice and dust. There are 13 known rings around the planet.

Oberon

Umbriel

Miranda

Uranus

Ariel

What Are Uranus's Moons?

Uranus has 27 known moons. One moon has very deep grooves. It is called Miranda.

Miranda

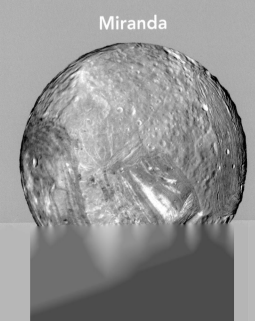

Who Discovered Uranus?

William Herschel discovered Uranus in 1781. He found the planet by accident.

18

How Is Uranus Different from Earth?

All planets spin. Uranus spins differently than Earth. Uranus is the only planet that spins on its side.

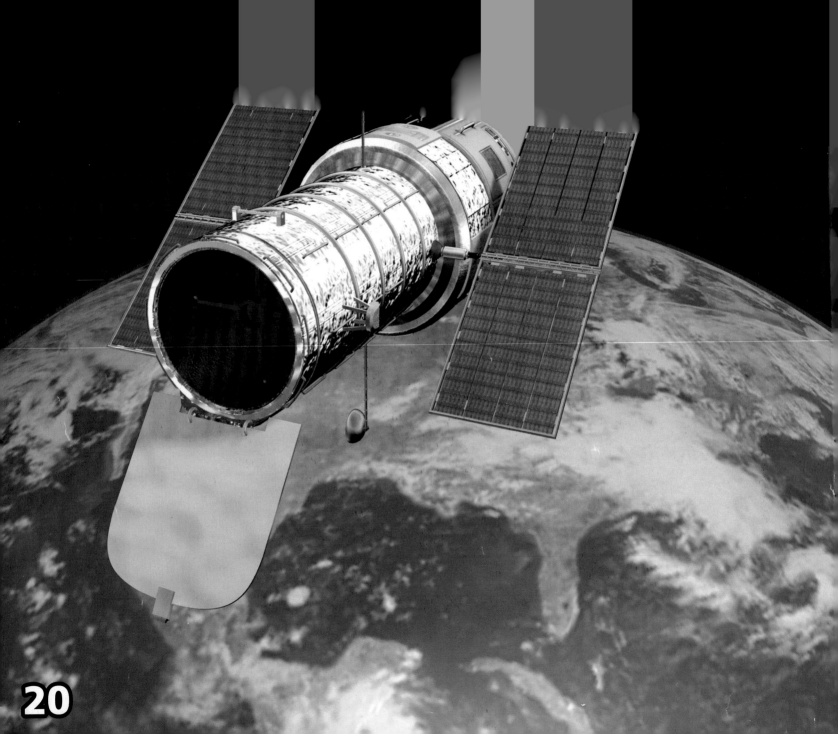

How Do We Learn about Uranus Today?

Telescopes make far away objects look closer. *Hubble* is a special space telescope. It has found two new moons around Uranus.

URANUS FACTS

This page provides more detail about the interesting facts found in the book. They are intended to be used by adults as a learning support to help young readers round out their knowledge of each planet featured in the *Planets* series.

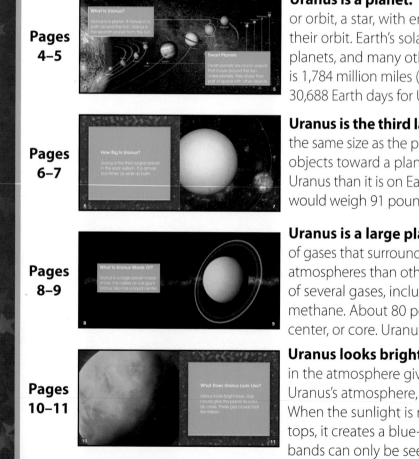

Pages 4–5

Uranus is a planet. Planets are round objects that move around, or orbit, a star, with enough mass to clear smaller objects from their orbit. Earth's solar system has eight planets, five known dwarf planets, and many other space objects that all orbit the Sun. Uranus is 1,784 million miles (2,871 million kilometers) from the Sun. It takes 30,688 Earth days for Uranus to make one orbit around the Sun.

Pages 6–7

Uranus is the third largest planet in the solar system. It is almost the same size as the planet Neptune. Gravity is a force that pulls objects toward a planet's center. The force of gravity is weaker on Uranus than it is on Earth. A 100-pound (45-kilogram) object on Earth would weigh 91 pounds (41 kg) on Uranus.

Pages 8–9

Uranus is a large planet made of ice. An atmosphere is made of gases that surround a planet. Ice giants have more ice in their atmospheres than other planets. The atmosphere of Uranus is made of several gases, including hydrogen, helium, and a small amount of methane. About 80 percent of Uranus's mass is contained in an icy center, or core. Uranus is the coldest planet in the solar system.

Pages 10–11

Uranus looks bright blue. Like the planet Neptune, methane gas in the atmosphere gives Uranus its color. As sunlight passes through Uranus's atmosphere, methane gas absorbs the red rays of light. When the sunlight is reflected back into space by Uranus's cloud tops, it creates a blue-green color. Uranus also has faint stripes. These bands can only be seen in enhanced images.

Pages 12–13

Rings make circles around Uranus. Scientists once believed that Saturn was the only planet with rings. In 1977, James Ludlow Elliot observed Uranus's rings blocking the light as they passed in front of a star. He was surprised to find them. Scientists have since discovered smaller rings within each of the 13 main rings. These are called "ringlets."

Pages 14–15

Uranus has 27 known moons. Scientists believe that most of Uranus's moons are made of equal parts rock and ice. Miranda has canyons that are 12 times as deep as the Grand Canyon on Earth. Miranda is only about 311 miles (500 km) wide and has very weak gravity. A rock dropped from Miranda's highest cliff would take a full 10 minutes to reach the bottom.

Pages 16–17

William Herschel discovered Uranus in 1781. He was working as an organist when he discovered the planet on March 13, 1781. In his spare time, Herschel built telescopes and studied the stars. Herschel's discovery made him famous. He quickly became the head astronomer for the king of England.

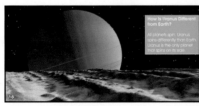

Pages 18–19

All planets spin. This is called rotation. Uranus spins horizontally on its axis, while Earth spins vertically. Scientists think that Uranus was hit by at least two large, planet-sized objects. This caused Uranus to shift 98 degrees onto its side. Scientists believe that the collisions happened billions of years ago.

Pages 20–21

Telescopes make far away objects look closer. Today, the National Aeronautics and Space Administration (NASA) uses the *Hubble Space Telescope* to take pictures of Uranus. These pictures show that powerful storms sometimes occur on the planet. Some of *Hubble's* other pictures show that Uranus's outer rings are brightly colored. Scientists are working on ideas for new space probes to send to Uranus.

KEY WORDS

Research has shown that as much as 65 percent of all written material published in English is made up of 300 words. These 300 words cannot be taught using pictures or learned by sounding them out. They must be recognized by sight. This book contains 60 common sight words to help young readers improve their reading fluency and comprehension. This book also teaches young readers several important content words. These words are paired with pictures to aid in learning and improve understanding.

Page	Sight Words First Appearance	Page	Content Words First Appearance
4	a, around, from, in, is, it, moves, the, what	4	path, planet, Sun, Uranus
5	are, of, other, part, that, their, they, with	5	dwarf planets, objects, space
6	almost, as, big, Earth, four, how, times	6	solar system
8	also, an, has, large, made	8	center, ice, ice giant
11	close, does, give, its, like, look, these, up	11	color, gas clouds, stripes
12	and, make, there	12	circles, dust, rings
15	one, very	15	grooves, Miranda, moons
16	by, found, he, who	16	William Herschel
19	all, different, on, only, side, than	21	*Hubble*, telescopes
21	about, away, do, far, learn, new, two, we		